IMAGES
of America

RANGELEY'S
HISTORIC LEGACY

The date and origin of this early map of the Rangeley region are unknown; however, it is possible that it was published by Charles A.J. Farrar, an author of several early books on the Rangeley region in the late 1880s and owner of the Jamacia Publishing Company. (Courtesy of the Rangeley Lakes Region Historical Society.)

ON THE COVER: This motorized toboggan was owned by Vernon Van Aken, who owned a camp on Mooselookmeguntic Lake. These men appear to be ready for a mail trip, as the attached sled appears to hold a mailbag. Their identities are unknown, but the man seated on the left may be John Kidder Sr., with Vernon Van Aken in front of him. Standing in the rear at left may be Vernon Stewart, owner of Hamm Garage Company. The man at far right is unidentified. (Courtesy of Jay Hoar.)

IMAGES
of America

RANGELEY'S
HISTORIC LEGACY

Gary Priest with the
Rangeley Lakes Region Historical Society

ARCADIA
PUBLISHING

Published by Arcadia Publishing
Charleston, South Carolina

Library of Congress Control Number: 2021951089

For all general information, please contact Arcadia Publishing:
Telephone 843-853-2070
Fax 843-853-0044
E-mail sales@arcadiapublishing.com
For customer service and orders:
Toll-Free 1-888-313-2665

Visit us on the Internet at www.arcadiapublishing.com

*This book is dedicated to the people of the
Town of Rangeley and its environs.*

CONTENTS

ACKNOWLEDGMENTS

The Rangeley Lakes Region Historical Society has been the recipient of two excellent postcard collections, one from Edward "Ebbie" Ellis and one from Montell "Gus" Hinkley. These are housed at the Rangeley History Museum on Main Street in Rangeley. Together, these collections total over 4,000 postcards and are one of the greatest resources available to provide such a rich visual history of the area. Not to be forgotten are the many camp owners who recorded life at their summer cottages over the years. I have been extremely fortunate to review several of their albums and to acquire copies of many photographs that are included in this pictorial history of the Rangeley area. And then there are the numerous year-round residents who loved to take photographs of their homes, businesses, and places of employment as guides and caretakers. These items provide an excellent resource for anyone doing research on the Rangeley region. I am totally indebted to the society for access to this rich collection of memorabilia. Without their wholehearted support, this book would never have been possible. All images with no designation are courtesy of the Rangeley Lakes Region Historical Society.

As a lover of Rangeley history, I have been collecting old photographs of Rangeley for many years. Unfortunately, many of the donors are now unknown, so they remain designated as (AC), or author's collection. My apologies to them, and I hope they will enjoy the results of my efforts. All other images from the author's collection are also designated as AC.

There are many photographs where I do know the donor and am happy to recognize them here: Vanessa Adams, David and Peter Beisler, Michael Blythe, Dennis Breton, Dan Case, William Chapman at the Bethel Historical Society, Thomas Doak, Arthur Douglass, Cindy Davis Fowler, Jay Hoar, John Kidder III, Skender Leidl, Monique Dumas Libby, Michael McCoy (the Emery Scribner collection), Everett Quimby, Stephen Richardson, Elizabeth Volckening, Sam Walk, Ann Taylor Wilbur, and Frances York.

INTRODUCTION

The town of Rangeley received its name in 1855 when it became an incorporated township. Prior to that time, it was referred to as the "Lake Settlement" or "the City." Around 1800, James Rangeley Sr., a mill owner in England, had acquired several thousand acres of land in what was then Massachusetts through the British Parliament. Upon his death, his son James Rangeley Jr. inherited the land. James Jr. arrived in the settlement in 1825 with his family (wife Mary, two sons, and three daughters) to see the land that he had inherited. He found that several families (Hoar, Dill, Quimby, Rowe, and Toothaker) had already settled and built homes on his land. Rangeley was not upset to learn of these squatters and made arrangements for them to work for him in exchange for rights of ownership of the land. A large manor home of 12 rooms, with a porch the length of the building, was built facing the lake on a hill overlooking Oquossoc Lake (now Rangeley Lake) about two miles west of the current downtown business area. A well was also dug next to the house. (A section of the house and the original well are still there in 2022; however, that section of the house has been moved about 200 yards east).

Disaster struck the family on Christmas day in 1827 when the oldest daughter, Sarah, died at the age of 19. Rangeley's wife, Mary, struggled to adapt to life in the wilderness and never really recovered from Sarah's death. She was used to the finer things in life, which she had enjoyed in England. Residents of the area readily accepted the Rangeley family, and James invested his own money to build a grist mill at the outlet of Oquossoc Lake, thus enabling the local population to eliminate the 40-mile round trip to Phillips to have their grain ground into flour. He also built a sawmill to prepare lumber for local use, and paid to build a new road to Phillips, reportedly in the amount of $30,000 (about $946,000 in 2022). Soon the locals began referring to James Rangeley as "Squire Rangeley" and to the town itself as "Rangeley." In 1841, the family abandoned life in the wilderness and moved to Phillips, later to Portland, and eventually resettled in Virginia. There, Rangeley built another large estate, and the area eventually became known as Rangeley, Virginia. Some of his descendants still live there, and in 2005 when Rangeley, Maine, celebrated its 150th birthday, several members of the family came to town to participate. An exhibit on the family, which they presented to the town, is now on display at the Rangeley History Museum.

The Rangeley region has been a destination area since 1818, when Luther Hoar built a cabin on the shore of Oquossoc Lake and moved his family there. He was soon followed by several other settlers before James Rangeley and his family arrived in 1825 to claim the land that his family had acquired. By midcentury, the town of Rangeley had become a destination. In the 1850s, David Pingree and Ebenezer Coe bought thousands of acres of timberland in the area and built several dams to hold back the water in the lakes until the spring floods arrived to float their timber downstream to the mills on the Androscoggin River. Then, in the 1860s, George Shepard Page took eight brook trout weighing a total of 51.875 pounds home to New York City, which was, naturally, written up in the New York papers, encouraging the arrival of fishermen to the area. Accommodations were now required to house them, so several hotels and fishing camps were built. Families soon joined the fishermen to enjoy the cool mountain weather, and larger hotels became the norm. The arrival of the railroad in 1891 created a big resort building boom, which lasted into the 1920s.

Between the Great Depression, the 1935 floods (which wiped out several railroad bridges), and World War II, expansion was brought to an abrupt halt. After the war, there were major changes: automobiles became accessible to more households, new highways were constructed, and travel across the nation became available to the entire population. Rather than spend an entire vacation in one place, people "hit the road." Motels and motor courts sprang up, and the old hotels became relics of the past and were razed or burned. With the passing of the hotels, their properties were sold and subdivided and individual summer residences appeared. In the 1960s, skiing was introduced at Bald and Saddleback Mountains, followed by snowmobilers. All-terrain vehicles soon arrived to take advantage of the expanded snowmobile trails. Today, with the expansion of the internet and the availability to work from home happening across the nation, Rangeley is once again a destination.

The old adage "a picture is worth a thousand words" is never more truthful than when producing a history such as this. An image of a subject eliminates all conjecture as to what was actually there at a given point in time. Locating old photographs of buildings in Rangeley has always been a challenge since so many of the early photographs concentrated on the numerous sporting camps and fishing. And so it should have been, as these images were the first public relations program to make the outside world aware of the beauty of Rangeley and its fabulous fishing waters. However, it is often the photographs that you don't have or cannot recover that make an interesting topic. In this case, it is images of the early schools and mills that are missing in most collections.

In this book, there are some new topics that have never received their share of attention in previous histories of Rangeley. Logging was the first industry to attract businessmen to the area in the 1850s, creating the need for dams to be built to raise water levels to float the logs to mills downstream. Steamboats also played a very important role in transportation from 1876 to about 1935, as well as for private pleasure. Winter scenes have rarely been emphasized, and the Civilian Conservation Corps's history in Rangeley has never been published. It is extremely pleasing to include these subjects in this book. As for hotels and scenes from the past, these have been the focus of the author's interest for many years, and several new photographs have been included in this publication.

One

THE STEAMBOAT ERA

The steamboat era in the Rangeley area began in 1876 when the state passed legislation giving Charles W. Howard exclusive rights to operate watercraft propelled by steam on Rangeley Lake for five years. In a separate act, Charles A.J. Farrar was given exclusive rights to operate on the Richardson Lakes for five years. The following year, Fred C. Barker obtained exclusive rights to navigate Mooselookmeguntic and Cupsuptic Lakes for five years. Elmer Thomas obtained exclusive rights to Kennebago Lake in 1883 for seven years.

Charles Howard operated the *Oquossoc* for one year on Rangeley Lake and then sold it to Fred Barker. Howard then built the *Mollychunkamunk*. The Rangeley Lake Steamboat Company was formed in 1891 and operated three steamers: *Irene*, *Mollychunkamunk*, and *Florence Percy*. In 1896, the *Irene* burned and was replaced the following year by the *Rangeley*. The *Rangeley* burned in May 1898, but fortunately, a new steamer, *Christine*, was launched later that month. Hartry Field, Daniel Field, and James W. Brackett bought the company in 1901, including the steamers *Christine* and *Comet*, and the following year launched a new *Rangeley*, the largest steamer in the region.

After Fred Barker purchased the steamer *Oquossoc* in 1877, he operated it on Mooselookmeguntic Lake between Bemis, Upper Dam, and Haines Landing. During his career, Captain Barker owned the steamers *Metalluc*, *Mollelocket* in 1886, *Mollychunkamunk* in 1889, the *Florence E. Barker* in 1896 (named after his daughter and the largest in his fleet), and the *William P. Frye* in 1903. The last two were much larger than the earlier ones. Barker's fleet also included the *Oozalluc*, which was in operation in 1896.

The Richardson-Rangeley Lakes Transportation Company operated three steamers on the Richardson Lakes: the *Olivette*, the *Mollychunkamunk*, and the *Welokennebacook*. Not surprisingly, the latter were the Indian names for these two lakes. The company also operated two steamers on Umbagog Lake: the *Diamond* and the *Parmachennee*. In 1887, the Androscoggin Lakes Transportation Company took over and added a new steamer, *Capt. Farrar*.

On Kennebago Lake, Captain Thomas operated the *Reindeer*, which ran from the outlet down the lake to the Kennebago Lake Hotel. By 1889, it was replaced by *Kennebago* and was operated by the Richardson brothers, owners of the hotel at Kennebago.

In addition to these public steamers, there were several private steamboats operating on all the lakes. Unfortunately, very few photographs of them are available; therefore, there is little mention of them here. The death knell for the steamboat era came in 1935 when spring floods washed out railroad bridges on both lines serving Rangeley and severed all rail transportation to the area.

The steamer *Rangeley* is tied up at the wharf in Oquossoc. The wharf was located where the Oquossoc Marina wharf is in 2022. The captain is believed to be Harry Soule. (AC.)

The steamer *Rangeley* is arriving at the Mountain View Hotel dock. Steamers generally operated from Greenvale to Rangeley and on to the Mountain View Hotel at the outlet of Rangeley Lake. The season began with "ice out" and continued into October.

Billy Soule bought his own steamer in 1889, had it hauled from Phillips to Rangeley by a team of eight horses, and christened it *Cupsuptic*. In 1892, he bought a new steamer and named it *Maysie*. It is not known which steamer this is.

Steamer Kennebago, Lake Kennebago, RANGELEY, Maine

The little steamer *Kennebago* is shown at the wharf at Kennebago Lake Hotel. In 1901, it made two trips daily down the lake. It was also available for excursions; however, "it must not interfere with the Beaver Pond buckboard or cause the captain to be late for dinner," according to one advertisement.

Captain and engineer licenses were issued by the State of Maine on an annual basis. Here is a copy of the engineer's license issued to Fred C. Barker in 1921, certifying his qualifications as an engineer. (Courtesy of Stephen Richardson.)

The steamer *Rangeley* is tied up at the town wharf at the foot of Lake Street about 1910. On the left is the Ernest Haley Boathouse, and in the rear are Marble Station, the Rangeley Lake Hotel, and the Rangeley Motorboat Boathouse.

Charles A.J. Farrar founded the Richardson-Rangeley Lakes Transportation Company in 1876. He was later honored by having this steamer named after him. Originally, service was from South Arm at the lower end of Lower Richardson Lake to Upper Dam. It was later expanded to the head of Upper Richardson Lake at Mill Brook and terminated at the private camp of J.L. Whittier, known as Birch Lodge. (Courtesy of Bethel Historical Society.)

One of the steamers for the Rangeley Lakes Steamboat Company is tied up at the wharf at the Mountain View Hotel. The large building in the background is the boathouse at Lake Point Cottage, a private camp. (Courtesy of Elizabeth Volckening.)

RICHARDSON (RANGELEY) LAKES
STEAMBOAT COMPANY
SUMMER SEASON 1881.

Steamboat Service on the Richardson Lakes.

One of the new and elegant Steamers **WELOKENNEBACOOK** or **MOLECHUNKAMUNK,** will commence their regular trips on the Richardson Lakes, as soon as the ice goes out, connecting with the teams from Andover, steamers DIAMOND or PARMACHENEE on Lake Umbagog, and the steamers on the Upper Lakes.

TIME TABLE.—Leave Middle Dam for Metallic Point, Mosquito Brook, and Upper Dam at 8 A. M. Leave South Arm at 1 P. M. for Middle Dam, Metallic Point, Mosquito Brook, Upper Dam and Mill Brook. Returning, leave Upper Dam at 10 A. M., for Mosquito Brook, Metallic Point, Middle Dam and South Arm. Leave Upper Dam at 4 P. M., for Mosquito Brook, Metallic Point and Middle Dam.

RATES OF FARE.

South Arm to Middle Dam.... ..$0.50 | Middle Dam to Head of Lake...$1.00
South Arm to Upper Dam........ 1.00 | South Arm to Head of Upper
Middle Dam to Upper Dam....... 0.75 | Lake.............................. 1.50

The Steamers may be hired for Excursion Parties at reasonable rates, when not engaged on regular trips.

ROUND TRIP TICKETS.

Boston to Middle Dam and Return *via* Bryant's Pond (Rail, Stage and
  Steamer)..$13.00
Boston to Upper Dam and Return, *via* Bryant's Pond (Rail, Stage and
  Steamer).. 14.00
Boston to Indian Rock and Return, *via* Bryant's Pond (Rail, Stage and
  Steamer).. 15.25
Boston to Indian Rock, *via* Bryant's Pond and Andover; Return, *via*
  Rangeley, Phillips and Farmington............................ 15.25
Boston to Magalloway and Return, *via* Bryant's Pond (Rail, Stage and
  Steamer).. 16.50
Boston to Upper Dam and Dixville Notch and Return, *via* Bryant's
  Pond (Rail, Stage and Steamer).............................. 20.50
Boston to Upper Dam, *via* Bryant's Pond, Return *via* Dixville Notch
  (Rail, Stage and Steamer)................................... 17.75

The above Tickets are $1.00 less where parties go between Boston and Portland, each way, by Steamer.

PRINCIPAL BOSTON TICKET OFFICES.—Grand Trunk Railway Ticket Office, 280 Washington St.; Boston & Maine Railroad Depot, head of Washington Street (Haymarket Square); Eastern Railroad Depot, Causeway St., opposite Friend; Lowell Railroad Depot, Causeway Street; B. C. & M. & W. M. R. R. Ticket offices, No. 5 State Street, and 240 Washington Street; and Portland Steamers, India Wharf.

NEW YORK.—Grand Trunk Railway Ticket Office, 1285 Broadway, and Offices of Providence and Fall River Lines Steamers.

PHILADELPHIA.—Any regular Ticket Office of the Pennsylvania, or Philadelphia and Reading Railroads.

BALTIMORE and WASHINGTON.—Any regular Ticket Office of the Pennsylvania Railroad.

Each year, steamboat companies issued new schedules. This is a schedule of operation for the steamboats plying the Richardson Lakes in 1881. (Courtesy of Bethel Historical Society.)

This is one of Captain Barker's steamboats tied up at Haines Landing on Mooselookmeguntic Lake around 1910. The landing was in front of the Mooselookmeguntic House.

HAINES LANDING, MOOSELOOKMEGUNTIC LAKE, RANGELEY REGION, MAINE   1336

Upper Dam was often a meeting point for steamers transporting people and goods on Mooselookmeguntic Lake. From this point, they could walk across Upper Dam, down a short path to the steamer wharf on Upper Richardson Lake, and sail up or down on the Richardson Lakes. The steamer on the left is the *Florence E. Barker.*

Steamboat Landing, Rangeley, Maine.

The wharf at the foot of Lake Street in Rangeley was the major terminal for the Rangeley Lake Steamboat Company. Behind the large steamer is the ticket office and on the right is the home of Julia Dill, a well-known fly tier. To the right of the Dill house is Capt. Ernest Haley's boathouse, and the large building behind it was the home of Phineas Richardson.

Ed Coburn operated Middle Dam Camps, known as Lakewood Camps after 1909. He later acquired his own steamer, *Helen*, from J. Parker Whitney and utilized it to transport his guests to and from his establishment. The *Helen* burned and sank in July 1946. (Courtesy of Bethel Historical Society.)

The A.E. *Rowell* was a flatbottom sidewheeler owned by the Berlin Mills Company and was used as a towboat to haul boomed logs on the Richardson Lakes. It was built in Portland in 1927 and shipped in sections by train to Bemis. The sections were transported over the ice to Upper Dam and assembled there. When its life ended, it was hauled onto the shore near Mill Brook and cut up for its metal. (Courtesy of Bethel Historical Society.)

The steamer *Olivette* was part of the fleet owned by Captain Barker. Here it is tied up at the Upper Dam wharf with the Upper Dam House and cabins in the background. (Courtesy of Bethel Historical Society.)

Billy Soule, the owner of Pleasant Island Camps, has one of his steamers tied up at the wharf at his camps on Cupsuptic Lake. Soule used his steamers to pick up guests arriving at Haines Landing and transport them to his resort at Pleasant Island on Cupsuptic Lake.

There was a train station at South Rangeley with a steamboat landing. Passengers arriving on the Rumford Falls & Rangeley Lake Railroad could get off there and transfer to a steamer that would take them to several destinations on Rangeley Lake, either hotels or private camps.

Rangeley Steamboat Co.,
RANGELEY, ME.

HEWEY & CLARK'S
Mail Line.

Unequaled Equipments,

Close Connections,

Good Speed

Hewey & Clark's line of steamers on the Rangeley Lake will be run during the season of 1891 strictly for the accommodation of patrons. Tourists can be accommodated at any time of day or night. The following table gives the running time of the regular boat:

Rangeley for Mountain View and the Outlet at 7 A. M., arrive at 8 A. M. Leave the Outlet and Mountain View for Rangeley and Greenvale at 10.15 A. M., arrive at Rangeley 11 15, Greenva'e 12 M.

Leave Greenvale at 1.30 P. M., arrive at Rangeley 1.50. Leave Rangeley at 2 P. M., arrive at Mountain View and the Outlet at 3 P. M. Returning, leave 5.45, arriving at Rangeley at 6 45.

The Florence Percy is kept in readiness for the use of pleasure parties at all hours and can be run to all points on the lake. For further particulars address

F. C. HEWEY, or S. E. CLARK
RANGELEY ME.

This advertisement was placed in the *Phillips Phonograph* of May 22, 1891, by Frank C. Hewey and Sam Clark, who had just bought the Rangeley Lake Steamboat Company and were readying for the coming season. The steamboat companies always arranged their schedules to coincide with the arrival of the trains in Rangeley and Oquossoc. (AC.)

The *H.P. Frost* was prefabricated in Portland in 1923, shipped by rail to Bemis, and reassembled there. It was a flat-bottomed sidewheeler measuring over 120 feet long that was used to tow logs on Cupsuptic and Mooselookmeguntic Lakes. After it went out of service, it was towed to the shore of Cupsuptic Lake and abandoned. This photograph of its remains was taken in the 1950s. (Courtesy of David and Peter Beisler.)

The steamer *Diamond*, also owned by the Brown Company, operated on Umbagog Lake. It was assembled in Errol, New Hampshire, and launched on the Androscoggin River. It was used to tow log booms across the lakes.

The steamer *Henry B Simmons* was the first steamer on the Richardson Lakes, being launched in 1876. The ticket price from Boston to Upper Dam and return was $16 via Andover, Maine. The traveler went by rail to Canton, Maine; by stagecoach to South Arm on Richardson Lake; and by steamer to Upper Dam.

Sam Betton, the owner of Bellevue camps, near Upper Dam on Upper Richardson Lake, had his own wharf and a small steamer called *Wawa*. It burned in June 1891. (Courtesy of Bethel Historical Society.)

In the winter, steamboats were housed in large boathouses. One of the largest, storing two steamers, was at the Rangeley Lakes Steamboat Company's boathouse. Here, the steamer *Rangeley* is being launched in the spring from the boathouse just west of the current Episcopal church parking lot. (Courtesy of Vanessa Adams.)

The *Rangeley* is shown leaving the wharf at the foot of Lake Street in Rangeley. The section of the town seen behind the steamer includes the buildings at the foot of Pleasant Street.

The current Loon Lodge was built in 1909 for Elizabeth Ludeke as a private home, which she named Weduba. She and her husband were ardent fishing people. They had many visitors, who all arrived by steamboat in the early days. (Courtesy of Elizabeth Volckening.)

The steamer *Rangeley* is tied up at what the photograph says is the "outlet" of Rangeley Lake. It was actually the steamboat landing at South Rangeley, as there are railroad tracks leading right onto the dock. According to geologists, there had been an outlet near that end of the lake centuries ago.

Steamer Landing, Upper Dam, Me.

This photograph was taken in 1914 and shows the steamer landing at Upper Dam. The long building in the background parallel to the dam is where the dam keeper controlled the raising and lowering of the gates that regulated the flow of water through the dam.

The Rangeley Lake Steamboat Company was formed on February 1, 1900, by Hartry Field, Daniel Field, and James W. Brackett. This is a certificate of shares of stock issued to James Brackett. The company was dissolved in July 1937 as steamboat travel was abandoned by the public. The company's two remaining steamboats, *Rangeley* and *Oquossoc*, were hauled up on the shore of Rangeley Lake and intentionally burned.

This is the timetable issued by the Rangeley Lakes Steamboat Company for the summer of 1913. Steamboat companies advertised extensively in the newspapers and sportsmen's magazines to attract customers to the Rangeley area.

The State of Maine required annual inspections of the hull and boilers of all steam-driven vessels. Two men usually performed the inspections, one examining the hull and the other the boiler. This is the 1919 inspection certificate for the *William P. Frye*, one of Capt. F.C. Barker's steamers. (AC.)

During the Great Depression in the 1930s, several camps and steamers were abandoned by their owners. Steamers were often hauled up on the lakeshores and burned or left to rot. This is the hull of a small steamer on the shores of Cupsuptic Lake in fall 2003, when the water in the lake was very low. The closeup view below shows the deterioration of the steamer over the years. The engine had been removed, possibly by antique or junk collectors. (Both, AC.)

Rangeley Lakes Steamboat Co.

SUMMER ARRANGEMENTS 1899.

Steamers will leave Rangeley at *7.30 a. m.,
2.00 and *3.30 p. m., for Mingo, Mt. View, Rangeley Outlet and the lower lakes.
7.30 a. m. trip connects with Capt. Barker's steamers for the Birches, Bemis, Upper and Middle Dams. 2.00 and 3.30 p. m. trips for the Birches and Bemis.
All trips connect with Billy Soule's steamers for Pleasant Island and Cupsuptic Lake.
Returning leave Rangeley Outlet and Mt. View House at *10.00 a. m., 2.45 and *4.30 p. m., or on arrival of Capt Barker's steamers.
Summer boarders' tickets good for ten trips over this line will be sold for $2.50.
Single fares, 75 cts. Guides' fares, 25 cts.
Steam Launch for charter.

C. W. HOWARD, Manager.
*Mail trips.

Barker's Steamers,

Mooselookmeguntic Lake.

SEASON OF 1899.

My steamers, Florence E. Barker, Metalluc and Oozallic will take passengers to all points on the lake, making close connections with trains on Rumford Falls & Rangeley Lakes railroad and all steamers on Rangeley and Richardson lakes.

CAPT. F. C. BARKER, Proprietor.

Also proprietor of Camp Bemis and the Birches.

This steamer, one of those operated by the Androscoggin Lakes Transportation Company, is approaching the landing at Middle Dam Camps on Lower Richardson Lake. Steamers from this company made regular trips between South Arm Landing and Upper Dam.

These advertisements by the Rangeley Lakes Steamboat Company and Captain Barker show their schedules for the coming summer. They appeared in the *Phillips Phonograph* on June 6, 1899. (AC.)

The Barker Hotel was the headquarters for Captain Barker's steamboat fleet. This photograph was taken at the Barker wharf with two of his steamers tied up there. One of the steamers is building up steam to head out on a trip up or down Mooselookmeguntic Lake.

Wharf and View from Lakewood Camp, Middledam, Rangeley, Maine.

The camps at Middle Dam were renamed Lakewood Camps in 1909 by owner Ed Coburn, who operated them until he died in 1943. He later bought his own steamer, *Helen*, which is probably the small steamer tied up next to the large steamer here.

Capt. Ernest Haley sits at the helm of his boat *Lillian*, which he built in 1913. In the background is the footbridge going from the foot of Lake Street to the Rangeley Lake House. The large house on the right was the home of Phineas Richardson.

One of the Kennebago Lake steamers is towing a canoe down the lake about 1915 and appears to be launching a rowboat into the lake for fishermen. The lake is five miles long, and many of the favorite fishing spots were at the opposite end.

Two

ACCOMMODATIONS AND EARLY TOURISM

The early accommodations in the region were limited. The Indian Rock Hotel, later the Greenvale House; John Burke's Tavern; Hinkley's Hotel, later the Rangeley Lake House; Camp Henry, later Mountain View Hotel; Angler's Retreat, later Lakewood Camps or Middle Dam Camps; and Upper Dam Camps were all providing lodging in the 1860s. It was not until the 1870s, when word about the big fish was published in the New York newspapers, that fishermen started to arrive in large numbers. The next 30 years saw a boom in hotel construction in the region with over a dozen additions.

Steamboat travel was introduced in 1876 and made traveling from lake to lake much easier. In June 1891, the Phillips & Rangeley Railroad, a narrow-gauge line, began operating between Phillips and Rangeley, and in 1902 the standard gauge Rumford Falls & Rangeley Lakes Railroad was extended into Oquossoc. Soon, the fishermen were bringing their families and servants and staying for two weeks, a month or two, or the entire summer.

The Great Depression and World War II led to the demise of the big hotels: help was not available, visitors diminished due to the loss of the trains and the rationing of gasoline, and everyone concentrated on the war effort. Some hotels managed to stay open, but some closed for the duration of the war. After the war, many of the tourists never returned, and in the 1950s, many hotels closed for lack of business, were torn down, or burned.

Second homeowners now dominate the scene in Rangeley. The desire of many people to leave cities for rural areas, the reopening of Saddleback Mountain ski area, and the introduction of faster internet service are attracting increasing numbers of tourists and new year-round residents. There are only five of the old hotels operating today: Bald Mountain Camps, Rangeley Inn, Lakewood Camps, Grant's Camps, and Bosebuck Mountain Camps.

This is the first view that early travelers from Madrid would have had of Rangeley Lake (upper left) in the 1800s. The farm in the center later became the Greenvale House. Note that the early road to Rangeley does not follow the lakeshore but goes inland up over Dallas Hill.

The Greenvale House, at the junction of Route 4 and South Shore Road, was originally known as the Indian Rock Hotel prior to 1871 and was the first accommodation available after leaving Madrid. After Henry Kimball acquired it, he changed the name to Greenvale House. With the arrival of steamboats in 1876, a walkway was built from the hotel to the landing. The house burned in 1895 and was never rebuilt.

This is the site of the first hotel in downtown Rangeley. Originally, it was known as Hinkley's Hotel, operated by Eben Hinkley. It burned in the fire of 1876, and the structure pictured, built a year later, was named the Rangeley Lake Hotel. In 1895, John and Ella Marble moved the main structure about a quarter-mile to the lakeshore and built additions on each end.

The Oquossoc House (two-story building on left) was built in 1877 by Abner Toothaker in downtown Rangeley. It was on the lot between the current Morton & Furbish Real Estate Company and the Skowhegan Bank. Ed Grant was the manager for several years. John and Ella Marble bought this hotel, used it as an annex to the Rangeley Lake House, and kept it open all winter. It burned after 1911.

George Soule built a large cabin near the outlet of Rangeley Lake and called it Camp Henry. He sold it to Henry Kimball in 1876, who tore down the old cabin and built a new hotel that he called Mountain View House.

Henry Kimball built the Mountain View House in 1878. It was a two-story building with about 20 rooms. In 1895, an annex was added that contained a huge fireplace. Another addition was added in 1902. In 1952, it was sold, the main hotel was torn down, and the annex was converted into a dining room and cocktail lounge. The annex burned in August 1956, and the land was subdivided. (Courtesy of Cindy Davis Fowler.)

Either Joshua Rich or his brother William built the first camps at Middle Dam around 1860 for fishermen and called it Angler's Retreat. The camp was a short walk from Middle Dam, where there was excellent brook trout fishing. Some early travelers reached this destination via Lake Umbagog and then up the Rapid River rather than by boat from South Arm at the foot of Lower Richardson Lake. (Courtesy of Bethel Historical Society.)

A new hotel was opened in 1878 and operated by Aldana Brooks and Horatio Godwin. Ed Coburn took over in 1893. Around 1909, he changed the name to Lakewood Camps and ran it until he died in 1943. A fire in 1957 destroyed the main lodge and several cabins. They were quickly rebuilt, and operations continued as usual. This is one of the five old resorts still operating today in the Rangeley area. (Courtesy of Bethel Historical Society.)

The original Upper Dam Camp was built in the 1850s and consisted of two buildings. A new hotel was erected between 1881 and 1886, and several individual cabins were later added. All the hotel property was leased from the Union Water Power Company, owners of the dam. Brookfield Energy owns the property today. The Grant family operated it for over 50 years. The hotel closed in 1952 and was demolished in 1958. (Courtesy of Bethel Historical Society.)

In 1921–1922, a dance hall known as the Casino was built just south of the Upper Dam. It became immensely popular, and camp owners and their guests on the Richardson Lakes and Mooselookmeguntic Lake went there by boat to enjoy dancing. During the winter, it was used to store boats and canoes. When the Upper Dam House was razed, the Casino was also torn down.

The Kennebago Lake Camps were first known as Forest Retreat and built by George Snowman in 1871–1872. Ed Grant, Phineas Richardson, and Cornelius Richardson bought the property in 1879 and built this lodge. In 1888, they moved the hotel away from the lake to higher ground.

This aerial view shows the location of the hotel after it was moved and many of the individual camps. The hotel closed in 1972, and the contents were sold at auction. Two years later, the property was subdivided and the camps were sold individually.

Every morning, numerous guides would meet at the various hotels to guide their "sports." Not all guides would have a job for the day; thus, they would remain at the dock in case an angler showed up and needed a guide. This group, with the Mooselookmeguntic House in the background, is obviously enjoying a day off from guiding.

This is the Mooselookmeguntic House, some of the camps, and the waterfront in 1915. The hotel had about 20 rooms and there were 27 cabins as part of the complex. The hotel burned in 1958, and all the cabins were converted to housekeeping cabins. The property was subdivided in 1986, and the cabins were sold individually.

Pleasant Island, Camps

Billy Soule, son of George Soule who operated Soule's Camp, constructed three cabins on Pleasant Island in 1884, and by 1911 had 24 cabins on the island and the mainland. (Courtesy of Cindy Davis Fowler.)

THE ISLAND — PLEASANT ISLAND LODGE

Billy Soule built a 300-foot bridge to connect the camps on Pleasant Island with those on the mainland. Several of the camps and the dining room burned in 1961. The dining room was then relocated to the mainland, and the bridge fell into disrepair and was eventually removed. In 1985, the camps were sold at auction.

Capt. Barker's Camps at Bemis, Me.

In 1880, Fred Barker purchased land and camps from the railroad at Bemis at the lower end of Mooselookmeguntic Lake. He tore down the old camps and erected seven cabins and a dining hall. Over the years, he built several additional camps. He sold them in 1928 to Frank Savage, and they operated until the late 1950s, when they were sold individually. A part of the dining room was struck by lightning in 1959 or 1960 and burned. (Courtesy of Cindy Davis Fowler.)

This shows the dining room behind what is known as Cleft Rock. It has now been converted into a private camp and was still there in 2022. The story is that Captain Barker slept between these rocks on his first night in Bemis.

The Birches. On Mooselookmeguntic Lake, Rangeley Lakes, Me.

The first camps on the island were built by Fred Barker in 1885, and he named them Students Island Camps. In the early 1890s, Barker changed the name to The Birches. In 1896, he built eight new cabins, and by 1925, the number of cabins had reached 28. The hotel and 11 cabins were destroyed by fire in 1925, and the remaining camps were removed to the Barker. (Courtesy of Cindy Davis Fowler.)

The Office and Main Camp at the Birches, Mooselookmeguntic Lake, Me.

This building at The Birches housed the office, kitchen, dining room, two bedrooms downstairs, and four bedrooms upstairs. It burned in 1925 and was never rebuilt.

The first camps on Loon Lake were built in 1889 by Jerry Oakes and Roland York and named Forest Camps. Seven years later, York bought Oakes's share and renamed the camps York's Log Village. Additional cabins were built over the years until the number reached 30. They remained in the York family into the 1960s, when the property was subdivided and the cabins were sold.

J. Lewis York built the main lodge in 1930. It contained the office, dining room, and kitchen with a piazza around three sides of the building. It had the largest indoor fireplace in the region. The female help stayed in the several rooms over the kitchen. This building is still standing in 2022.

Bald Mountain Camps, Me.

Bald Mountain Camps opened in 1897 with seven cabins that could accommodate 40 people. In December 1914, a fire destroyed several camps. They were quickly replaced along with a new dining room and kitchen. Ronald and Rose Turmenne acquired the camps in 1942, and their grandson Steve Philbrick and his son operated them in 2021. The cabins have been winterized, and the dining room is open year-round today. (Courtesy of Cindy Davis Fowler.)

Wharf at Bald Mt. Camps, Rangeley, Me.

This is a view looking north from Bald Mountain Camps in 1914. The large building behind the man standing on the dock was the summer home of Aurelius S. Hinds and was called Lagamonte.

The Mingo Springs Hotel opened in 1896 with a dining camp and five sleeping camps. In 1906, the small dining camp was demolished, and the hotel shown was built. (AC.)

This photograph shows the Mingo Springs Hotel and its waterfront in the 1940s. The structure on the far left, Rosecliffe, was built in 1902 as a residence for James Munyon, the owner. The hotel and Rosecliffe were razed in 1964, and all the debris was hauled onto the ice and burned. The land was subdivided, and the camps were sold individually. (AC.)

A group of fishermen bought from Cornelius Richardson the camps where the Kennebago River enters Cupsuptic Lake in 1868. The following year, they erected the main building, which contained a kitchen, dining room, and a combined sleeping area/lounge with a piazza across the front. In 1870, the Oquossoc Angling Association was incorporated and remains in existence today.

Here is an early view of the sleeping area and lounge room with its large fireplace. As the years went by, members built their own cabins with kitchen facilities, and the kitchen eventually closed. Today, this room is a dining room/ recreation area.

The Barker, Mooselookmeguntic Lake, Me.

The Barker was the last of Fred Barker's hotels and the largest. The three-story structure with a cupola was built in 1902 and contained 30 rooms. The following year, he added a casino, and several camps were later constructed. The hotel was razed in the summer of 1967, the property was subdivided, and the cabins were sold. (Courtesy of Cindy Davis Fowler.)

The steamboat landing at the Barker was the gathering place where the local guides met their sports in the morning to take them fishing. The guides who did not have work for the day often hung around the dock passing the time of day hoping a late-arriving sport would appear, looking for a guide.

Grant's Camps were built in 1904 by Will and Hall Grant with their father, Ed, joining them the next year. All the lumber to build the camps had to be rowed down the lake, as there was no road to the camps. A fire in May 1977 consumed the dining camp and several cottages. All were immediately rebuilt, and the camps are still operating in 2021.

Rufus Crosby was a Rangeley guide and is seen here at Grant's Camps inspecting and getting the Rangeley boats ready for spring fishing. Crosby also operated a garage in Rangeley for the repair of automobiles. (Courtesy of Dan Case.)

In the early 1900s, a footbridge was constructed over Haley Pond Stream at the entrance to Rangeley Lake. This enabled Rangeley Lake Hotel guests to walk to the village by crossing Haley Pond Stream to Lake Street. In the background, the center portion with the cupola was the original Rangeley Lake Hotel that was first located where the Rangeley Inn sits in 2021. The additional wings were added in 1896 and 1908.

This aerial view of the Rangeley Lake Hotel reveals its immense size, with 175 rooms and a dining room that could seat 300 guests. The land behind the hotel is a nine-hole golf course.

The Rangeley Tavern Corporation was formed in 1908, and the following year opened this three-story hotel. About 1925, the owners acquired the neighboring structure (far left), originally known as the Frazar Inn. It was then moved and annexed to the tavern, thus nearly doubling its room capacity. In 1947, the name was changed to the Rangeley Inn. In recent years, the inn has been significantly remodeled and remains open year-round.

The front desk area of the Rangeley Tavern was finished with birch paneling and remains the same today as in this photograph. This is the only operating hotel in the Rangeley area whose lobby has not been remodeled.

DINNER

FRIDAY, AUGUST 4, 1905

Puree of Green Peas · Tomato Soup

Queen Olives · Pearl Onions · Lettuce

Saratoga Chips · Celery · Sliced Cucumbers

Baked Chicken Halibut, Allamande Sauce

Boiled Corned Beef and Cabbage

Boiled Cincinatti Ham Tartar Sauce

Roast Spring Lamb, Mint or Brown Sauce

Prime Ribs of Beef, Dish Gravy

Fricassee of Chicken

Honeycomb Tripe Fried in Batter

Rice Fritters with Maple Syrup

Boiled Onions · Marrow Squash · Green Peas

Boiled and Mashed Potatoes · Stewed Tomatoes · Steamed Rice

Baked Indian Pudding Hard or Cream Sauce

Snow Pudding, Custard Sauce · Fresh Raspberry Whips

Fresh Blueberry Pie · Apple Pie · Squash Pie

Chocolate Ice Cream

Ribbon Cake · Ginger Wafers

Grapes · California Plums · Watermellon

Mixed Nuts · Dates · Layer Raisins

Coffee · Milk · Tea

American Roquefort, and Edam, Cheese

Soda and Bents Water Crackers

Iced Tea · Iced Coffee

Domestic Ginger Ale 13c   Imported Ginger Ale 25 c   Apollinaris 25 c.

The Water used in this Hotel for drinking and cooking purposes
is from the famous Rangeley Spring.

RANGELEY LAKE HOUSE

Seen here is a menu from the Rangeley Lakes Hotel from Friday, August 4, 1905. It shows a wide variety of items available for a hotel located in the wilds of Maine. Many of the vegetables, milk, and eggs were provided by local farmers.

Frank Case, owner of the boathouse next to the Rangeley Lake Hotel, acquired the hotel and property in 1957. He held a gigantic auction and sold anything that people would buy, from room keys, beds, silverware, dishes, doors, bathtubs, sinks, and more. In the fall, he hired a company to tear down the building. The property has been subdivided and now contains several homes. (Courtesy of Dan Case.)

John Danforth built Camp Caribou on Parmachenne Lake about 1870, and it became an elite fishing camp. In 1890, Henry Wells and a group of New York friends bought the camp and renamed it the Parmachenne Club. It consisted of a main lodge, kitchen, maid quarters, guide quarters, and 13 individual cabins. The Brown Company acquired it in 1945, and President Eisenhower stayed here on his 1955 visit. It is now privately owned.

Henry and Sherman Pickford built their first camp in 1898 on Rangeley Lake, and in 1900 added four more cabins and a main lodge housing a dining room and main office. Harry Look operated these camps from 1924 to 1943, and his son ran them until 1959. They were sold after that season and remained in operation until 1972 as housekeeping cabins. The buildings and contents were auctioned off in 1975, and the land was subdivided and sold.

Hotels and Camps

HOTEL.	PER DAY.	RATE PER WEEK.	PROPRIETOR.	P. O. ADDRESS.	
Hotel Rumford,	$2.00 to 2.50	Special.	G. A. Ames,	Rumford Falls,	Me.
The Barker,	2.50 to 3.50	"	F. C. Barker,	Bemis,	"
Camp Bemis,	2.00 to 3.00	"	" "	" "	"
The Birches,	2.50 to 3.50	"	" "	" "	"
Upper Dam House,	2.00	"	Chadwick & Co.,	Upper Dam,	"
Bald Mt. Camps,	2.00 to 3.00	$12 to $16	Amos Ellis,	Bald Mountain,	"
Mooselucmaguntic House,	2.00 to 3.50	Special.	T. L. Page,	Haines Landing,	"
Pickford's Camps,	2.50	"	H. E. Pickford,	Rangeley,	"
Pleasant Island Camps,	2.00	$12 to $15	Billy Soule,	Haines Landing,	"
Mt. View House,	2.00 to 3.00	Special.	L. E. Bowley,	Mt. View,	"
Rangeley Lake House,	2.50 to 5.00	"	John B. Marble,	Rangeley,	"
Anglers' Retreat,	2.00	$12 to $15	E. F. Coburn,	Middle Dam,	"
The Maples,	2.00	$10.50	Drew & Scamman,	Weld,	"

It was very common for the railroads to publicize hotels at their destinations. This is from a Maine Central Railroad brochure published in 1910. It lists the hotels and camps in the area along with their prices, proprietors, and addresses.

Ed Grant built camps at Beaver Pond in 1876–1877 and named them Beaver Pond Camps. Beaver Pond is about eight miles north of Little Kennebago Lake. The camps were later known as Seven Pond Camps, and in 1910 were sold to the Megantic Club. These fishermen may have had a long wait for mail to be delivered to this post office, as it was deep in the wilderness of Maine.

Three

THE LOGGING INDUSTRY

David Pingree of Salem, Massachusetts, had made a fortune in the shipping trade out of Salem, and around 1850 was looking for a new venture. He purchased all the land from Lower Richardson Lake to Kennebago Lake for its timber. Beginning in the late 1840s, he built a series of dams between the big lakes to increase the water flow in order to move timber from the Rangeley region to the mills on the Androscoggin River. Upper Dam was at the outlet of Mooselookmeguntic Lake, Middle Dam was at the outlet of Lower Richardson, Lower Dam (also known as "Pond-in-the-River Dam") was on the Rapid River, and Errol Dam was on the Androscoggin River. In 1877, Pingree sold the dams to the Union Water Power Company in Lewiston, Maine.

The Berlin Mills Company, later the Brown Company, acquired much of the land in the Kennebago Lake area all the way to the Canadian border shortly before 1860. Most of the early woodcutters were French Canadians and worked in teams of two with a pair of horses. One cutter would fell and limb the tree, hitch the log to a horse, and send the horse and log to the yarding area. The second cutter would cut the log into four-foot lengths and stack it. The horse then returned to the first cutter, passing the second horse, which was dragging another log in the opposite direction down to the second cutter. Scalers then arrived to measure the number of logs cut, and branded each log for identification. When the spring melt came and the rivers were raging, the logs were pushed into the river and sent downstream to the mills in Rumford and others farther downstream.

From the 1870s to the 1940s, many of the local guides turned their efforts to lumbering in the winter. Over the years, there were several small logging operations run by local businessmen. Among them were Huntoon and Therrien (often referred to as "Hoot & Toot"), run by Hayden Huntoon and Charles Therrien. Later, Donald "Bart" Morton had logging operations in several areas in the region.

The Hudson Pulp and Paper Company had lumber operations in the Saddleback area in the 1940s and 1950s cutting softwood for its mills. This pulpwood was moved to the South Branch of the Dead River and floated to the Kennebec River and on to the mills on that river.

In 1920, there was a huge lumbering operation at Kennebago Lake. This pile was about a quarter-mile north of the dam and powerhouse. The logs were pulled out of the river, put on a conveyor that ran at a steep incline, and dumped. The logs were later loaded into boxcars and shipped to the International Paper Company mill in Rumford.

This photograph is of the American Realty Company logging camp at Kennebago in 1920. The building on the right is the kitchen, and on the left is the dining area.

This man, known as the scaler, is demonstrating the use of a walking wheel caliper. This tool measured the length and diameter of a log. The scaler would use these numbers to determine the volume of lumber in the log. These calculations determined the number of board feet that could be produced at the sawmill. Cutters were usually paid on the basis of the volume produced. (Courtesy of John Kidder III.)

Rangeley natives Hayden Ross and Sam Dunham are standing beside their log sled loaded with birch logs. A load piled high like this was often referred to as a "bully load."

A log hauler is sitting atop a load of long logs with his team of horses in Redington around 1900. Horses were the mainstay of many farmers and loggers, and were well treated. The loss of a horse or team was an economic disaster and could deprive the owner of a way to make a living.

A small dam was built at the outlet of Beaver Mountain Lake (then known as Long Pond) in 1901, which raised the level of the lake by about two feet. Logging operations were conducted in the area in 1904 by a man named Otis. All logs would have been sluiced through the dam in the spring and floated to Rangeley Lake, then boomed down the lake to the outlet.

In the early 1900s, Bemis was a thriving lumber village with two mills, a railroad, a steamboat landing, several homes, and a school. These are some of the buildings along the shore with the International Paper Mill in the rear. The mills and most of the buildings in Bemis were destroyed in a huge fire on August 1, 1921. (Courtesy of Cindy Davis Fowler.)

This is a closer look at the International Paper Company mill with its stacks of logs at Bemis. C.B. Cummings built a birch dowel mill in 1901 that operated until it burned in 1921. It employed over 100 people and used nearly 5,000 cords of birch each year. The foundations of these mills are still visible between Bemis Road and the lakeshore even though the area is heavily overgrown. (Courtesy of Cindy Davis Fowler.)

The men with the long poles ("pickpoles" in logging vernacular) are sluicing logs through Haley Pond Dam in early 1900. The woman posing for the photographer is unidentified. The large building in the background is the Frazar Inn, which was later added as a wing to the Rangeley Tavern.

A logger has just felled a yellow birch tree and stacked the tools of his trade. One- and two-man crosscut saws were used to fell hardwood trees, and axes were used to trim off the branches. (Courtesy of Everett Quimby.)

Loggers seldom worked alone in the woods, as there were several different tasks to perform from felling the tree, trimming off the limbs, and hauling them to a yard. This crew has chained several logs together, and the horses will haul them to a log yard to be loaded onto a truck. (Courtesy of Dan Case.)

John Kidder Jr., with the peavey, and his brother Harland "Spike," with the pulp hook, are moving logs into the river to begin their journey to a mill. The onlookers in the rear are Jim and "Bud" Wilcox, and in the lower right is Dr. Paul Fichtner, all from Rangeley.

In the 1930s and 1940s, Saddleback Mountain was logged heavily. A train of loaded logging sleds has just arrived at Saddleback Lake from the wood yard on the side of Saddleback Mountain. (Courtesy of Jay Hoar.)

These logs are awaiting the spring thaw and will be floated down the South Branch of the Dead River. In the background is a new train of logs arriving at the lake. (Courtesy of Jay Hoar.)

The area near the bridge over the Dead River on Route 16 near the Redington turnoff was the collection area for pulpwood in the 1960s. Each year, thousands of cords of pulpwood were neatly stacked along the riverbank awaiting the spring runoff. (Courtesy of Michael McCoy.)

The melting snow from the mountains, which created huge volumes of water in the rivers, was the usual method of transporting logs to the mills. Bulldozers were used to push the stacks and piles into the river. Crews followed the logs downriver to release log jams, and later, cleanup crews waded into the river pushing stray logs along. (Courtesy of Michael McCoy.)

Log Boom 1924

In the 1920s, trucks dumped hundreds of cords of pulpwood onto the ice in front of what is now the Town and Lake Motel in Rangeley. The logs were surrounded by a boom, and once the ice melted, were boomed down the lake to the outlet. This operation was phased out in the mid-1950s. (Courtesy of John Kidder III.)

Alvin Lombard, a blacksmith from Waterville, Maine, built 83 Lombard haulers between 1901 and 1917, which were used extensively in the Rangeley region. Their primary use was to pull up to eight loaded log sleds; however, some were used to move logs in the mill yard such as this one at the Kempton Lumber Company in Rangeley.

These logs have been sluiced through Upper Dam and have created a log jam just below the dam. The river driving crews were responsible for clearing these jams and often had to use dynamite to release the logs. These men probably had the most dangerous job in the logging industry.

Local men either owned their own log trucks or hired them from a business that provided them. They usually worked as a one-man crew, loading the truck by hand, driving to the destination, and once again unloading by hand. This photograph shows Arno Spiller loading his truck.

Calvin Putnam and Henry Closson bought Redington Township in 1883 for its lumber. Putnam founded the Phillips & Rangeley Railroad, a narrow-gauge line, and laid tracks to haul in supplies to build two mills. The depot is on the left, and the "big" mill is on the right. Here the logs were sawn into boards and hauled by train to Putnam's shipyard in Danvers, Massachusetts. (Courtesy of Guy Roux.)

This is a view of the village of Redington, sometimes referred to as "Sawdust City," about 1895. The village even had its own school for the workers' children. The population was estimated to be about 270. The mill closed in 1902. There were only two small buildings here in 2021, and the entire area is under the control of the US Navy, which uses it for survival training.

Bridge maintenance was a very important function during the hauling season. Jack Haley stands by his overturned log truck at South Bog Stream after the bridge he was crossing collapsed.

In 1943, logs were dumped onto Haley Pond, sluiced through the dam into a log boom on Rangeley Lake, and towed down the lake to the outlet in Oquossoc. Thin ice was always a hazard. This truck owned by Huntoon and Therrien fell through the ice and had to be rescued. The house in the background is at the corner of Pond and High Streets in Rangeley.

This log railway was constructed somewhere south of Parmachenne Lake and was used to move supplies and equipment to the logging camps and then to transport logs on the return journey. George Soule of Rangeley is in the front, and his son Eugene is in the rear. (AC.)

This image shows a photographer with his camera on the logs talking to another man while standing on the floating logs in the winter of 1917–1918. Logs were retained in a millpond until they were ready to be sawn into lumber. (Courtesy of John Kidder III.)

This logging crew is enjoying their lunch deep in the woods. The man with the coffee pot was probably their boss. (Courtesy of Jay Hoar.)

In 1910, the Berlin Mills Company and International Paper Company built a dam at Parmachenne Lake to control the water flow in order to move cut logs down the Magalloway River to their mill in Berlin, New Hampshire. It was later abandoned, and today there are only a few base logs remaining. It is now a favorite fishing spot for anglers who can access this gated area.

The original Upper Dam was built in 1853 by Coe & Pingree to assist in floating logs to the mills downriver. It was over 1,500 feet long with logs bolted together containing stone ballast, which raised the level of Mooselookmeguntic Lake 9–15 feet. In 1884, the dam was rebuilt, raising the level of the lake another 8–10 feet. In 2016–2017, Brookfield Energy replaced it with a new dam. (AC.)

A boom of logs has been towed across Mooselookmeguntic Lake, and these men are using pickpoles to push them through a channel to be sluiced through Upper Dam.

This is the entire Redington Mill crew in front of the big mill in the late 1890s. The mill was built in 1891, with all the lumber being cut on the top floor. The equipment included two band saws, a gang edger, a planer, a matcher, and a clapboard and shingle machine. The mill was closed and dismantled in 1902 and rebuilt at Toothaker Pond in Phillips, Maine.

These men are moving pulpwood into the Dead River at a place about two to three miles beyond the Lower Dallas bridge on Route 16, where the road was high above the river. Trucks would pull over to the side of the road and the drivers would heave each log over the bank, creating a huge pile. It was not unusual to have over 5,000 cords of wood along the riverbank.

Two men with their team of horses are hauling a sled of pulpwood along a trail through the woods. The trails would be built in the fall but were not usable until enough snow had fallen to cover the stumps and rocks left in the trail. (Courtesy of Thomas Doak.)

In the 1920s, this river driving crew is having lunch along the banks of the river where they are working. River drivers pushed logs into the river and later followed them downstream, onshore and in bateaux, refloating the logs that were hung up along the shore and breaking up log jams in the river. The latter often required blasting them out with dynamite. (Courtesy of John Kidder III.)

The Kennebago Dam was completed in 1916 and began providing electricity to Rangeley with John Madden as its first superintendent. In 1917, it was incorporated as Oquossoc Light and Power Company, with H.A. Furbish as president. The power company merged with Central Maine Power in 1976, and the dam was sold to private individuals. (Courtesy of Thomas Doak.)

The Berlin Mills Company had three Lombard haulers at Kennebago in Stetson Township, with two haulers operated on a daily basis and one kept in reserve in case of a breakdown. The early haulers pulled three sleds of logs, and later models were designed to pull eight sleds, replacing approximately 60 horses.

Sawmills located on a lake or pond usually kept their logs in a holding area known as a millpond. They moved the logs into the mill via a conveyor to be sawn into lumber. These men are at the millpond at the Bemis mill. (Courtesy of Cindy Davis Fowler.)

The Kempton Lumber Company mill in Rangeley is seen from the Baptist church steeple in the 1930s. G. Lafayette "Lafe" Kempton built the mill in 1901 and operated it by steam. It burned in 1915 but was rebuilt and operated into the 1950s. Note that the hill behind the mill, known as "Cemetery Hill," is devoid of trees while Bald Mountain is in the distance. (Courtesy of Jay Hoar.)

Four

WINTER SCENES

During the heyday of hotel operations in Rangeley, most photographs were taken in the summer. Most visitors had no idea how their summer hosts spent the winter or realized the amount of work that had to be done to maintain the camps and provide them their comforts in the summer. New camps would be built, old camps refurbished, wood was cut for the summer fires, ice was harvested to refrigerate foods and cool drinks, and boats were repaired and painted. Many of the guides picked up their axes and saws and joined the many lumbering operations each winter. Life was not easy for the people of Rangeley, but they persevered.

Life was not all work. They still found time for outdoor recreation such as sledding, tobogganing, ice skating, iceboating, sleigh rides, snowshoeing, skiing, and horse races on the ice. Some of the residents were very inventive and created early versions of snow machines and used them to reach and inspect their outlying camps, where they usually had to clear the snow load from the roofs.

In the early 1900s, snow arrived much earlier and accumulated to greater depths, and the lakes and ponds froze over by Thanksgiving. An article in the *Phillips Phonograph* in mid-December 1906 stated that there were over three-and-a-half feet of snow on the ground, people were shoveling off their roofs, and all the icehouses had been filled. Today, the lakes rarely freeze before the end of December, and skiing is possible on Saddleback Mountain in December only because of snowmaking equipment.

This view of Main Street in Rangeley on December 11, 1900, looks toward the current Rangeley Inn. The large building in the center is the Frazar Inn. The left side of the photograph shows a house where the old IGA building stands today.

The snowbanks were high along Main Street in the 1940s. It was not until the early 1950s that the town began removing snow in front of all the stores. The building in the center was the M.D. Tibbetts hardware store on the corner of Main and Pond Streets.

A recent snowstorm has buried Main Street. The town tractor is attempting to widen the road by pushing back the enormous snowbanks. The J.A. Russell Hardware Store is on the far right.

Traveling by horse was the main mode of transportation for some people. This man is on his horse in front of Riddles Drug Store. Note the height of the snowbanks.

J. Lewis York, owner of York's Log Village at Loon Lake, used his sled dog team to traverse the five miles to town in the 1920s. Here he is shown on Main Street with the Baptist church in the background. (Courtesy of Frances York.)

Two reindeer are pulling a sled on Rangeley Lake in the late 1930s or early 1940s. The sled appears to be the same model as those in use today. (AC.)

Wintertime is a great time to view many of the summer homes around the area. Snowmobile trails use many of the lakes and ponds as connectors throughout the trail network. This is the former Camp Skedadler on Kennebago Lake, with the boathouse decorated with moose antlers. (AC.)

John Burke and E.A. Rogers built the first store here in 1875. It was enlarged in 1891 with the addition of a second-floor auditorium where town meetings and dances were held, and where the first silent movies were shown. It was called the Big Store. The building later became the offices for the Rangeley Express Company operated by Emile Carrignan. It was located where the Rangeley Inn parking lot is today. (AC.)

Sledding was a popular adult sport in the 1930s and 1940s. These people are sledding at the Van Aken cottage on Mooselookmeguntic Lake in March 1943. From left to right are Peggie Van Aken, Ray Harnden, Hayden Huntoon, Ferne Kidder, Florence Harnden, and John Kidder Sr. (Courtesy of John Kidder III.)

Eugene Herrick operated a dry goods store with apartments on the second floor on Main Street just south of Depot Street. The building was relocated prior to the construction of the new Phillips & Rangeley Railroad depot in 1909.

Autos left on the highway were buried under huge snowbanks when the roads were plowed (no different from today). The Rangeley Inn is in the background. (Courtesy of Jay Hoar.)

Ken Lizotte's Foodland was in the former J.A. Russell hardware building. Tony Jannace later acquired the building and operated a food store. The building burned to the ground in a spectacular fire in 1995. The current building is the home of the Rangeley Friends of the Arts theater. The building on the right is Riddle's Pharmacy. (Courtesy of Michael Blythe.)

These men are at the beginning stages of cutting ice on Haley Pond. In the background is a ski slope/toboggan run. Local teenagers used to build small ski jumps on this hill. (AC.)

Sleigh rides were a popular Sunday afternoon pastime, and these people are all bundled up in their fur coats to enjoy the ride. This sleigh is passing in front of the Rangeley Tavern. (Courtesy of John Kidder III.)

Snowshoeing was a popular Sunday pastime for the locals. The men at the lumber camps worked from sunrise to sunset six days a week. On Sundays, family members and friends often visited the camps bringing food not offered in the camp dining room. This large group is shown at one of Hayden Huntoon's lumber camps in the 1920s. (Courtesy of John Kidder III.)

Axel Tibbetts owned a garage and taxi business on the corner of Center and Main Streets. It previously had been the Grange Hall and later housed the town offices. In the 1950s, the Boy Scouts held their weekly meetings on the second floor. This building was razed in 1961, and Dom's Auto was located there in 2022. (Courtesy of RHS.)

This motorized toboggan was owned by Vernon Van Aken. In the 1940s–1950s, when deep snow blocked the road to Phillips, this was used to haul the mail until the road was opened. (Courtesy of Jay Hoar.)

J. Lewis York, owner of Loon Lake Camps and the Kennebago Lake Hotel, built this machine in the 1930s to travel from Loon Lake to Kennebago Lake to check on his property. During his visits, he was most likely clearing snow from many of the camp roofs. He also would have used this vehicle to travel the five miles from Loon Lake to Rangeley. (Courtesy of Frances York.)

Sid Harden was a guide and later became a game warden. He also owned camps at Long Pond. This is a vehicle that he converted into a snow machine by removing the front tires and replacing them with skis and placing tracks over both sets of wheels. (AC.)

This iceboat, located on Haley Pond in the 1950s, was stored on weighted nail kegs when not in use to avoid having to dig it out after a snowstorm. It was owned by Verd Tibbetts, owner of M.D. Tibbetts & Sons Hardware store, located just out of sight on the left. The building directly behind the iceboat is the Richards Hunger woodturning mill, now the Ecoplagicon Nature Store. (AC.)

The stretch of road just beyond the scenic overlook on Route 4 heading toward Phillips was notorious for its huge snowdrifts from the westerly winds blowing down Rangeley Lake. At times, snow would be so deep and hardpacked that it was necessary to use hand power to open or widen the road.

This photograph of the IGA was taken in 1968, decorated for the Christmas season. In the 1940s, Bert Herrick operated a trading post selling antiques at this location. Chester Johnson constructed a new grocery store here in 1950. It was later purchased by Milford Taylor and the IGA moved here from what is now the Red Onion. (Courtesy of Ann Taylor Wilbur.)

The building was originally known as the Kodak Shop and was owned by Sherman Hoar from 1919 to 1949. It then became a drugstore until 1964 when it was sold to Ramona Oakes, who named it Mo's Variety. A generation of kids growing up in Rangeley remember the store for its supply of penny candy. (Courtesy of Michael McCoy.)

This house was built on Pleasant Street about 1900 by Eugene Herrick and Ermon Toothaker and was owned by Hayden Huntoon when this photograph was taken in the 1930s. The barn seen here was removed many years ago. (Courtesy of John Kidder III.)

The Ellis Farm rope tow was installed in 1960 by the Rangeley Ski Club on Route 4 next to the current Farmhouse Inn (old Ellis Farm). Their purpose was to provide skiing opportunities for the youth in the elementary schools, and this program was the beginning of the after-school ski program. Roger Page was the instructor. After the 1962 ski season, the tow closed, and the program moved to Saddleback Mountain. (AC.)

J. Lewis York, the owner of York's Log Village, lived about a mile from his camps on a farm called Foxmoor where he raised silver foxes for fur. He was one of two fox farmers in the area, the other being Ray Fox. York is seen here on his bear paw snowshoes. (Courtesy of Frances York.)

A New Rangeley Sport.

Theron "T.J." Ellis was very ingenious and developed a new way to ride on the ice and snow. He is standing with a friend on Rangeley Lake in 1917 behind his Indian motorcycle sled. (AC.)

This horse appears to be harnessed to a sulky as it stands along the side of the Rangeley Inn. Several residents owned racing horses and even raced them on Rangeley Lake in the winter. (Courtesy of Jay Hoar.)

Winter traveling by auto was very difficult in the early days. Several residents rose to the challenge and made modifications to enable them to use their autos in winter. This vehicle is another example of how that was accomplished. (Courtesy of Frances York.)

The narrow-gauge line from Phillips to Rangeley, which opened in 1891, was constantly plagued with winter derailments. Ice would build up on the rails, causing the wheels to slide off, or deep snow would clog up the wheels and cause the same problem. If overloaded with logs, the cars would sometimes roll over when rounding curves. (AC.)

The Bald Mountain Ski Corporation, under the direction of Shelton Noyes, opened in January 1960 with a rope tow on Bald Mountain. The following year, the rope tow was replaced with a 2,300-foot T-bar lift. Gautier "Tibby" Thibodeau, the former owner of the Mooselookmeguntic House, stands by a sign advertising the area. The old ski lodge is now the home of the Rangeley Lakes Guides Association. (AC.)

In the winter of 1939, Hildegarde Watson hired S.A. Collins & sons to build this log camp on the east shore of Kennebago Lake just north of the Whitin/Lasell Camp. The logs were cut in Rangeley Plantation and hauled to this location, where they were peeled and cut to the required lengths. A unique feature of this camp is the arrangement of logs both horizontal and vertical. (AC.)

This is a view from the parking lot of Saddleback Mountain ski area in 1964 during its fourth year of operation. The lodge is in the background, with the mountain beyond. (AC.)

Sam York is pulling the ice saw on Rangeley Lake in the cove behind the current Episcopal church. In the early 1950s, the author worked for York, either working in the ice fields, pushing ice through the channel to the loader, or in the icehouse, packing the ice in sawdust. (Courtesy of Frances York.)

ICE CUTTING, RANGELEY LAKES, ME.

After an ice field has been laid out, a large circular saw is used to cut the ice to within two inches of the water. These men are using hand saws to cut the remaining ice. If the circular saw cut all the way through, the water would often refreeze before the ice cakes could be pushed to the loader. In the background is the Rangeley Lake Hotel.

Removing the hundreds of pounds of snow from cabin roofs was an annual task. In some places, the snow would drift several feet deep. These men are shoveling off a roof at Pickford Camps. (Courtesy of Sam Walk.)

Two people are dressed in bearskin coats to ward off the cold. The photograph was taken in the early 1900s at a camp owned by William Allen on the shore of Rangeley Lake in front of the current Country Club Inn. (Courtesy of Arthur Douglass.)

Ralph (left) and Fernald "Fern" Philbrick are standing by the deer they have recently killed. The photograph was taken at Camp Whatcheer at York's Camps on Loon Lake. The camp burned in 1932. (Courtesy of Frances York.)

Five

CHANGING TIMES AND THE LEGACY LEFT BEHIND

As time marches on in this world, many things change. Old buildings are removed to make room for more modern structures, old camps that had been neglected over the years or do not meet the comforts of the new owner are replaced by larger and more modern structures, and new businesses move into town as people relocate from urban areas to more rural settings. Much of this relocation has been made possible by the availability of high-speed internet service. And Rangeley is no exception. As the older generations pass on and take their knowledge of the Rangeley region, the younger generations would have no knowledge of many of the old landmarks without photographs to show them what existed years ago. This chapter is a tribute to their efforts to preserve the ever-changing history of our area.

The most notable transformation in the Rangeley area has been the change in accommodations. Beginning in the 1870s, large hotels and resorts with personal cabins and a central dining room were built on all the large lakes in the area. Fishermen flocked to these resorts in droves, and by 1900 were bringing their entire families for the summer. After World War II, the scene changed dramatically. Gas and automobiles became easier to obtain, the interstate highway system was begun in the 1950s, and people were anxious to travel after being confined to home during the war years. Many people no longer wanted to spend a week, two weeks, or more at the same resort, and motels were built to accommodate these travelers. The era of the large hotels came crashing down; the properties were subdivided and sold as separate lots.

In the 1970s, second homes became the new resorts. People became more affluent and could now afford their own hideaway. Winter sports made the Rangeley area a four-season resort area and the boom continues even today.

The beauty of the lakes and mountains continues to shine and welcome lovers of the outdoors. May it remain that way for many years to come.

Originally, there were two streams at the outlet at Haley Pond. They were replaced by the current dam about 1906. The first sawmill in Rangeley was built here in 1854 by Eben Rowe. The house on the left was built in 1900 and is where the author resided as a youth.

Frank Marchetti and his family stand in front of his store, next to what is now the Rangeley Lakes Region Historical Society's Rangeley History Museum. Marchetti moved here from Boston around 1900 and opened the Boston Store, which sold fruit, confectionery, tobacco, groceries, and crockery. The building later served as a restaurant, plumbing office, auto parts supply, and the office for the Oquossoc Light and Power Company. It was demolished in 1978.

On October 29, 1911, the still unfinished Rangeley High School erupted in flames and this is what remained after the fire was put out. The school was quickly rebuilt and opened for the spring term of 1912. It burned again the night of November 22, 1912, and once again, it was rebuilt. In 1927, it became an elementary school and remained in service until June 1975. The town office and town safety buildings are now located here.

In June 1918, Ira Hoar's livery stable burned and the flames jumped to the so-called "Big Store," officially the Oakes, Herrick, and Quimby store. The damage to the store was quickly repaired, and it reopened later in the summer. When the store went out of business in the late 1930s, the building became the headquarters for the Rangeley Lakes Motor Express. It was razed in 1965.

Ermon Toothaker and later Charles Case operated a grocery store here prior to 1919. It was sold to J. Sherman Hoar, who leased it to Albert Carlton. Carlton operated an ice-cream parlor for a few years in the 1920s in a building where the Backwoods store is in 2022, next to the Red Onion. Next to it on the right is the Kodak Shop. (AC.)

Hayden Huntoon is proudly sitting in the Rangeley Lake House mail delivery truck in June 1920. The vehicle was also used to transport hotel guests to various stores and other destinations. (Courtesy of John Kidder III.)

J. Lewis York, the owner of York's Camp at Loon Lake, had a second business venture: raising silver foxes for their fur. The pens were in a field behind his residence, which he called Foxmoor, about a mile from his camps. This venture ended with the start of World War II. Ray Fox was the only other person in the area to raise silver foxes.

In 1887, a trotting track was built on the farm of William Hoar at the top of the hill on Loon Lake Road on the right-hand side. Horse racing was a popular sport among many of the locals, and regular races were held here and occasionally on the ice of Rangeley Lake. The area has now returned to forest, but was there in the 1940s–1950s, when local children used the track to race their bicycles. In the 1970s, it was used as a race track for snowmobiles.

Fremont Davis bought the Rangeley Lumber Company property in 1961, tore down the old sawmill, and opened a marina on part of the land. The house on the right had a shop below, and the Davis family lived over it in the summer. A one-bay garage served as storage, and the two-bay building was the service area. (Courtesy of Skender Leidl.)

A band marches down Lake Street, probably soon after World War I. The houses on the left were all moved in the 1930s, when Harry Furbish purchased the land. In his will, he donated the land to the town, and it is now part of the Rangeley Town Park.

This store was built by Guy Pickel, a taxidermist, and opened in 1907. After he died in 1926, his wife, Arbeth, operated it until it was heavily damaged in a fire in 1965. The store sold hunting and fishing equipment and sportswear, and was decorated with many mounts on the walls. After the fire, the remains were cleared away, and an addition to the IGA was built. (Courtesy of Ann Taylor Wilbur.)

In 1889, Charles Barrett and Charles Belcher were building boats here on the south side of Main Street. Seven years later, Neal & Quimby were operating a grocery store here. In 1921, Sam and Clara Clark bought it, and she opened the Pine Tree Tearoom. In 1952, Lynn and Cecile Dumas took over and operated the Pine Tree Restaurant for nearly 40 years. The old building has been razed, and a residence has been built there. (Courtesy of Monique Dumas Libby.)

The Franklin Farmers Telephone Exchange was founded in 1913 and relocated to this building on Pond Street in 1925. The Rangeley exchange operated out of here until 1950, when the company was bought out by New England Telephone Company. It was operated by Prince and Helen Edwards for many years. (AC.)

The first train from Phillips to Rangeley arrived in June 1891 at this station. It was about 600 feet north of Main Street on Depot Street where there is a parking lot today. It was in use until 1906, when a new station was built closer to Main Street. (AC.)

The second Rangeley depot was built in 1906 on the west side of the junction of Main Street and Depot Street. It remained in use until the demise of the railroad in 1935 and was razed in 1938. (AC.)

PORTER AND QUIMBY'S CAMP, NEAR QUIMBY POND, RANGELEY LAKES, ME.
Photographed and Published by F. H. Hamm, Rangeley Lakes, Me.

Two Rangeley guides, Will Quimby and Frank Porter, had this camp in the woods north of Quimby Pond and used it as a retreat for their sports. Here, the guides and clients are with eight good-sized deer, typical for those days when there was no limit on deer.

This farm was on the north side of Routes 4 and 16, about halfway between Rangeley and Oquossoc. Austin Hinkley bought 196 acres in 1913 and probably built the farm. His widow, Edna, sold the house, barn, and all farm implements to Charlie Tobie in 1924. William Tobie took over on a foreclosure in 1929. During the 1930s, it was known as Lakemont Farm, and they rented rooms and cabins in addition to operating a large dairy farm. The barn and house burned in 1949, never to be rebuilt. (Courtesy of Charlie Tobie.)

Alice Fuller Davenport obtained property on Dodge Pond in 1920 and built a complex of camps facing west, all connected by a long piazza. Davenport traveled the world collecting antiques and named this place Trail's End. It was later owned by Joseph Bedell of Staten Island, New York. After he died in 1992, the camps were abandoned by his widow and fell into disrepair. All but one of the buildings have been torn down, and a new modern home is there today. (AC.)

Joel Wilbur of Phillips built this camp on the east shore of Rangeley Lake about 1873. His first trip to Rangeley was in 1845, to fish with his father. Here, he holds his catch for the day. The camp was later converted into a dining room for Birchwood Camps. It may have been the first summer camp on Rangeley Lake and was torn down in the 1950s. (AC.)

Lloyd Huntoon stands with his plane in front of the home of Mabel Case at the foot of Lake Street next to the town wharf in 1948. This was originally the home of Julia Dill, who tied and sold flies in the early 1900s. Case ran a laundry service from this house for many years. The house was razed in the 1970s. (Courtesy of John Kidder III.)

James Munyon built this lovely home in 1900. There was no road to the camp at that time; however, Munyon convinced the town to build a road, now Cottage Avenue, to the camp. In 1901, Munyon bought Mingo Springs Hotel, and in 1908 sold this house to Harriet Neher. The Nehers named it Kinnikinic, an Indian word for bunchberry. It was later owned by Robert Estes Sr., who tore it down in the late 1990s and replaced it with a more modern home. (AC.)

Arthur Gilman built the original cottage (on the left) in 1895 on the grounds of the Rangeley Lake Hotel and named it Rangemere. As the hotel expanded in size, Gilman desired more privacy and sold the cottage to the hotel, and its name was changed to Pawnee. The building was demolished in 1958. (AC.)

A welcome arch was located next to Salmon Ledge Camps in the 1930s. Three oil storage tanks were dismantled in Oquossoc and were to be shipped out of town; however, the arch was too low for the trucks to pass underneath. The first two trucks used the driveway at Salmon Ledge Camps to avoid the sign. The property owner, Annie Bok, grabbed a pillow and blanket and laid down in the driveway to prevent the passage of the last truck. Bok would not move, and the sign had to be torn down for the last truck to continue its journey. (AC.)

Zephie Andrews opened a small restaurant in the 1950s on Route 17 just south of Oquossoc village where people mainly ate in their vehicles. At that time, Duncan Hines was reviewing many restaurants, but not hers, so her motto became "the place Duncan Hines missed." Her specialty was a cheeseburger made with a large slice of cheddar cheese cut from a wheel. She died in 1957, and the new owner, Virginia Huntoon, changed the name to A&G Restaurant and specialized in fried clams. It was remodeled into a summer camp in 1982. (AC.)

This camp was built in 1912 and sold to Louis Gimbel in 1927. It was a large camp of 16 rooms with four fireplaces and was expensively furnished. There were two large stone pillars that held up the porch. It caught fire in June 1936 and burned to the ground. The Gimbels never rebuilt the camp, and later, the property became part of Pickford Camps. The two pillars are still there today. (AC.)

The house in the background is the focus of this photograph, not the horse and buggy. The house was built in the 1890s and was acquired by Urban Verrill in 1934, along with land on Haley Pond. Verrill opened Verrill's Deluxe Cabins in 1938 and operated them until 1968, when he sold them to the Rangeley Inn. The building was razed in 2021.

Joel Parker Whitney built this large two-story frame house on Upper Richardson Lake in the 1880s. Other buildings that were added later included a boathouse, woodshed, icehouse, dynamo and engine building, laundry, and guides' camp. Whitney became a wealthy man through sheep raising and mining in California and Colorado. He frequently traveled to Europe but always came to this camp every summer. After World War II, the contents were auctioned off, and the buildings were torn down. Today, there is a campsite here. (Courtesy of Bethel Historical Society.)

There were two signs like this welcoming visitors to Rangeley. This sign replaced the arch that was torn down in the 1930s and was near Salmon Ledge Camps on Route 4. It now rests on the porch of the Outdoor Heritage Museum in Oquossoc. (Courtesy of Sam Walk.)

Allerton Lodge was built in 1875 by Jeremiah Ellis for Reuben Allerton, a noted fisherman who chose the location because of the good fishing in the immediate area on Mooselookmeguntic Lake. He was also a founder of the Oquossoc Angling Association. An additional seven buildings were added over the years. The original building was razed about 2004, and a new modern lodge was erected. (AC.)

Camp Mitigwa was a boys' camp that opened in 1919 on Dodge Pond. It was accessible only by boat until 1953, when a road was built to the camp. Franklin Gray and Leon Nixon operated the camp from 1921 to 1966, and it accommodated over 100 campers every summer. It closed in 1972, and all buildings were demolished soon after that.

Arthur Gilman, who previously owned Rangemere, built this luxurious home on Rangeley Lake at what is now called Manor Point in 1900. Gilman was president of the Bradford Hat Company in Bradford, Massachusetts. Unfortunately, he died two years later, but his widow retained the property. In the 1920s, she added four camps, and she and her children operated a summer camp. Several children from Rangeley learned to swim at the camp. The main house burned in 1936 and was never rebuilt. (AC.)

Dr. John Wallace of Roxbury, Massachusetts, built these camps around 1922 on Bonney Point on Rangeley Lake and sold them to Alexander Dannenbaum of Philadelphia in 1928. Dannenbaum was the president of Pine Tree Silk Company. In 1956, it became a lodge with five housekeeping cabins; however, it lasted for only five years. The main lodge was torn down in the 1980s. (AC.)

William and Florence Cunningham built this beautiful log home in 1902 on Rangeley Lake and named it Loch Hame. All six buildings were connected by a covered piazza nearly 300 feet in length. Their daughter Fonda Hyatt inherited it, and it remained in the family until 1985. She maintained beautiful gardens all over the property. After the property was sold, the buildings were razed and the land was subdivided.

The Cunninghams were avid hunters and enjoyed traveling around the world on hunting expeditions. They decorated the interior of their camp with many trophy mounts. (AC.)

Arthur Gauthier, a Rumford businessman, built several camps on the west shore of Mooselookmeguntic Lake around 1910 and named them Wildwood. Fr. Eugene Trembly, his half-brother, was ordained into the priesthood in 1910 and loved to come to Wildwood to hunt and fish. He completed this chapel in 1919 and held the first service there on August 15 of that year. After he died in 1955, services were held only when a traveling priest visited. At right is an interior view of the chapel ceiling in 1988. Perpendicular log construction was used by Quebec pioneers in their earliest churches. Furnishings for the chapel arrived via train at Bemis and were rowed four miles across the lake to Wildwood. The chapel was removed in the winter of 1990, and the pieces were placed in storage in hopes it would be rebuilt, but it has not happened as of this printing. (Both, courtesy of Dennis Breton.)

Frederick Dickson's daughter Elizabeth Foster built Camp Anthony about 1900 and celebrated her honeymoon here. It was near Black Point on Rangeley Lake. Her husband, Maximillian Foster, was a journalist and writer and wrote many short stories and serials for the *Saturday Evening Post*. In 1912, they enlarged the camp and spent most summers there through the 1920s. Their daughter Elizabeth Foster Mann was the author of *The Islanders*.

Arthur Golder, a teacher, writer, and preacher, built the original camp on the south shore of Rangeley Lake, made mostly of cedar, in 1900. He utilized driftwood and tree stumps to build a unique stairway to the second floor. He sold the camp to B. Franklin Stahl, who was the resident physician at the Rangeley Lake Hotel for over 40 years. Stahl built two additional log buildings next to the old Driftwood Lodge in 1924. The original lodge was hauled down on the ice and burned in the winter of 1968–1969. (AC.)

Six

THE IMPACT OF THE CIVILIAN CONSERVATION CORPS

The Civilian Conservation Corps was established on April 5, 1933, by Pres. Franklin Roosevelt to provide much-needed jobs for men 18–25 years old. Each recruit was paid $30 per month and was required to send $25 of that home to help support their family. Meals, lodging, and work clothes were provided by the camp. There were ultimately 28 such camps in Maine, including the one in Rangeley. The Rangeley Camp, which housed the 144th Company, was in Greenvale, at the junction of Route 4 and South Shore Road about three miles south of Rangeley village. All recruits housed there were from Rhode Island. Enlistments were for six months and the recruit had the option to reenlist.

Life in the CCC was comparable to the US Army. The officers in charge were from the Army and were supported by local workers. A typical day started at 5:30 a.m. with "Reveille" and was followed by a hearty breakfast in the dining hall. Workers then collected their gear and were transported to their worksite by truck. They had a midday break for lunch at the worksite, and at the end of the day were trucked back to the main camp for an evening meal.

The company had eight stake-body trucks provided by the state and two canvas-covered two-and-a-half-ton trucks provided by the Army. Supplies, mostly food, were shipped by rail from Portland to Oquossoc and then hauled to the camp.

After-hours entertainment included football games between sections of the company, baseball games against other companies, swimming in the nearby Long Pond Stream, occasional trips into Rangeley for the movies, or visits to a local candy store or just laying around camp relaxing, reading, writing, or talking.

The recruits' first two projects were to build barracks for themselves and a fire lane to the top of Saddleback Mountain. Constructing fire lanes and trails on the many mountains in the area was a top priority. Other projects they completed were two 1,900-foot runways for an airport off of Loon Lake Road; the Wilson Mills Truck Trail, an extension of the road west from Pleasant Island to Wilson Mills (now Route 16); The Houghton Truck Trail, extending from Long Pond southwest by Four Ponds to join the current Route 17; Cupsuptic Truck Trail, a road north from the Cupsuptic Storehouse to Oxbow Township over to the Magalloway River and on to Canada; and several fire trails and picnic sites throughout the area.

The CCC camp closed in late 1938 or early 1939, and the property was sold to Harold Ferguson. None of the buildings are still standing.

When the first men arrived in the summer of 1933, there were no barracks or mess hall, and they lived in tents. Their first project was to erect barracks and a dining hall to house themselves before the winter snows and freezing temperatures arrived.

The early enrollees were required to build all the structures at the camp in Greenvale. This is the office building, which also included the blacksmith shop and tool room.

On the left is the main entrance to the CCC camp and in the center is the parade ground. As in the military, the day began at 5:30 a.m. with "Reveille," calisthenics, and a hearty breakfast before heading off to their worksites. A midday lunch was served at the worksite.

The camps were run by military officers and were operated accordingly. Pulling KP (kitchen police) duty was a regular assignment for the men and was done on a rotating basis. These men are peeling potatoes in the dining hall as part of their duty. All supplies were shipped from Portland to Oquossoc by rail and transported to the main camp by truck.

Most of the equipment used by the CCC was loaned to it by the state in which the camp was located. This is a gas-powered shovel operating at the Brown Company gravel pit.

Roads were built in summer and even in winter despite the cold and snow. The men were provided warm clothing and are seen here leveling a road with shovels. This is probably the Wilson Mills Truck Trail.

When heavy equipment was not available, the good old spade shovel was the most reliable tool available and was put to good use. These men are posing for one of their buddies, cameraman John Giacomini, with a half-shovel of dirt on a hot summer day.

It appears that the camp has just received a shipment of new beds and mattresses along with some new workers, judging by the trunks in the scene.

These are the types of dump trucks that were available to the men of the CCC. It is hard to say what they were planning to do on this winter day somewhere on Route 16 going toward New Hampshire.

The CCC had several outlying camps in the region, all made of logs. These men pose outside one after a day's work. If the worksite was distant from the main camp, the workers would remain there all week and return to the main camp on Saturday afternoon.

Horses were usually used to "twitch" logs out of the woods to the building site for the construction of barracks and a kitchen. They were also used to help clear logs and large boulders from the roadway and to drag the roads. Local residents were hired to perform those tasks and provided their own teams.

These are the type of dump trucks provided by the State of Maine. They are being hand-loaded by the men at a gravel pit.

These men are relaxing in their barracks. Each barrack was heated by three stoves, and the single-level bunks were arranged facing the center aisle. Organized recreation included football and baseball games, swimming in the river near the camp, and movies in town.

On a daily basis, many of the men were trucked out of the main camp to their worksite, which could be several miles away. This group of men is off to their worksite.

The dump trucks were much smaller in the 1930s and had far less horsepower than those built today. This truck is at a gravel pit and is being loaded the hard way—by shovel.

When dispatched to a gravel pit, the men often had to loosen the gravel bank using their pickaxes. Once the gravel was pried loose from the bank, it could then be shoveled into waiting trucks. This crew is posing with their pickaxes and shovels during a break.

These men are marching in a parade in Rangeley, possibly on the Fourth of July. The store in the background was the Clark Smith General Store, at the corner of Pleasant and Main Streets. The lot is now the parking lot for Morton & Furbish Insurance Company.

John Giacomini is shown on the left in 1938, along with his buddies having a good time at the gravel pit. He was 17 at the time, spent about 30 months in Rangeley, and donated several of the photographs in this chapter to the Rangeley Lakes Region Historical Society.

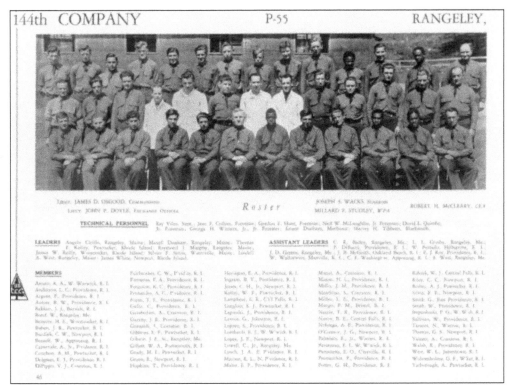

Lieut. JAMES D. OSGOOD, Commanding
Lieut. JOHN P. DOYLE, Exchange Officer
Roster
JOSEPH S. WACKS, Surgeon
MILLARD F. STUDLEY, WPA
ROBERT H. McCLEARY, CES

TECHNICAL PERSONNEL Ray Viles, Supt.; Jesse F. Collins, Forester; Gordon E. Hunt, Forester; Neil W. McLaughlin, Jr. Forester; David L. Quimby, Jr. Forester; George H. Winters, Jr., Jr. Forester; Lester Dunham, Mechanic; Harley H. Tibbets, Blacksmith.

LEADERS Angelo Cirillo, Rangeley, Maine; Manuel Dunham, Rangeley, Maine; Thomas F. Kelley, Pawtucket, Rhode Island; Raymond J. Murphy, Rangeley, Maine; James W. Reilly, Woonsocket, Rhode Island; Sylvio F. Sestito, Westerville, Maine; Lowdell A. West, Rangeley, Maine; James White, Newport, Rhode Island.

ASSISTANT LEADERS C. R. Bailey, Rangeley, Me.; L. L. Grubb, Rangeley, Me.; P. DiSicci, Providence, R. I.; W. Pentalle, Hillsgrove, R. I.; J. D. Green, Rangeley, Me.; J. B. McGrath, Oakland Beach, R. I.; E. J. Roy, Providence, R. I.; W. Waltierewce, Manville, R. I.; C. E. Washington, Apponaug, R. I.; J. West, Rangeley, Me.

MEMBERS

Amato, A. A., W. Warwick, R. I.
Andrikian, L. C., Providence, R. I.
Argent, F., Providence, R. I.
Autore, R. W., Providence, R. I.
Balduin, J. E., Bristol, R. I.
Bond, W., Rangeley, Me.
Bengton, H. E., Woonsocket, R. I.
Baban, J. B., Pawtucket, R. I.
Burdick, C. W., Newport, R. I.
Brunell, W., Apponaug, R. I.
Capecale, A., Jr., Providence, R. I.
Conghon, A. M., Pawtucket, R. I.
Deignan, F. J., Providence, R. I.
DiPippo, V. J., Cranston, R. I.
Fairbother, C. W., Prov'ce, R. I.
Fontanna, F. A., Providence, R. I.
Ferguson, K. C., Providence, R. I.
Fernandes, A. C., Providence, R. I.
Fopin, J. E., Providence, R. I.
Gallo, C., Providence, R. I.
Gustafson, A., Cranston, R. I.
Gazzty, J. B., Providence, R. I.
Gonzales, C., Cranston, R. I.
Gibbons, R. F., Pawtucket, R. I.
Gilson, J. E., W., Rangeley, Me.
Gilbert, W. A., Portsmouth, R. I.
Grady, M. F., Pawtucket, R. I.
Geane, R., Newport, R. I.
Hopkins, T., Providence, R. I.
Horrigton, E. A., Providence, R. I.
Ingram, H. V., Providence, R. I.
Jones, C. H., Jr., Newport, R. I.
Kahn, W. F., Pawtucket, R. I.
Langelone, E. R., C'tl Falls, R. I.
Langlon, S. J., Pawtucket, R. I.
Lapoulis, J., Providence, R. I.
Levson, G., Johnston, R. I.
Lepere, S., Providence, R. I.
Lombardi, F. C., W. Warwick, R. I.
Lopes, J. F., Newport, R. I.
Lowell, C., Jr., Rangeley, Me.
Lynch, J. A. E. Providence, R. I.
Macomi, R. L., N. Providence, R. I.
Maho, E. P., Providence, R. I.
Mimot, A., Cranston, R. I.
Mason, H. L., Providence, R. I.
Mello, J. M., Providence, R. I.
Marchom, A., Cranston, R. I.
Miller, J. E., Providence, R. I.
Morgan, P. M., Bristol, R. I.
Nazzie, T. R., Providence, R. I.
Narcy, B. E., Central Falls, R. I.
Nichonga, A. E., Providence, R. I.
O'Carney, J. G., Newport, R. I.
Palmisano, E., Jr., Warren, R. I.
Paratmeres, F. L., W. Warwick, R. I.
Perazketa, E. O., Cranville, R. I.
Pasmachia, P., Providence, R. I.
Potter, G. H., Providence, R. I.
Rabask, W. J., Central Falls, R. I.
Riley, C. C., Newport, R. I.
Rosho, A. J., Pawtucket, R. I.
Silvia, J. B., Newport, R. I.
Smith, G. Ros Providence, R. I.
Sorab, W., Providence, R. I.
Sapatkeski, P. G., W. Web, R. I.
Sullivan, W., Providence, R. I.
Tavares, N., Warren, R. I.
Thomas, G. S. Newport, R. I.
Vaiato, A., Cranston, R. I.
Walsh, R., Providence, R. I.
Wee, W. L., Jamestown, R. I.
Wolomsholmse, G. F., W'st, R. I.
Yadwinough, A. Pawtucket, R. I.

46

The men in this photograph were the commanding officers and their staff. Most of the technical personnel were from Rangeley or neighboring towns as well as several of the leaders and assistants.

One of the most significant projects in Rangeley was the creation of the first airport in town. The men of the CCC hacked two runways out of the forest on the Loon Lake Road about three miles from downtown. All stumps and rocks were removed, gravel was hauled in to level the runways, and it was considered an emergency landing field.

Horses, tractors, and road graders were employed to level the grade of the runway. In 2019, there was a major expansion that extended the main runway to 4,400 feet, allowing medical evacuation planes to service the area.

Before 1935, there was no road to Errol, New Hampshire, as the road ended at the entrance to Pleasant Island Camps. The CCC had the task of building a bridge over the Cupsuptic River and creating what is now Route 16 out of the wilderness. Here, the men are laying logs for the first pier on the eastern side of the river.

Occasionally during the winter, the blowing and drifting snow would make the roads impassable. The small trucks did not have the horsepower to move the snow, so towns resorted to human power to open the road. Here, men are clearing a section of Route 4 between Rangeley and Oquossoc.

The CCC also built and maintained several outlying camps, which reduced travel back and forth from the main camp. Pictured here are a log camp and cook room under construction at Toothaker Brook. The supervisors were generally experienced local carpenters and guides who doubled as contractors in the winter.

The main camp was at the junction of the current South Shore Drive and Route 4 in Greenvale, about three miles south of Rangeley. This photograph was taken early in 1934. The large building on the right is probably the kitchen and mess hall.

Wherever the CCC built trails or roads, there were always streams to cross, and the men became very adept in bridge construction. This bridge crosses Cold Stream. Another bridge was 80 feet long across the outlet of Saddleback Lake.

This shelter is at Cold Springs along the Dead River about eight miles east of Rangeley on the road to Stratton (Route 16). This area also provided camping facilities and was a popular place for the people of Rangeley to picnic in the 1940s and 1950s.

Bridge-building was a major accomplishment when trails and roads were being constructed through the woods and up mountains. This 80-foot bridge is over the outlet stream of Saddleback Lake that carried pulp logs down the mountain to Flagg Dam and on to the South Branch of the Dead River.

Road safety and reduction of forest fire hazards were two of the main concerns of the CCC. In several areas around Rangeley, the workers removed debris to create 50-foot-wide strips along each side of the highway. The clearing and pruning of trees gave motorists a clearer view of turns and bends in the road.

Work continued throughout the year, using whatever equipment was available. This gas shovel, on loan from the state, is being used to clear snow on the west side of the Cupsuptic River bridge, now Route 16. On the north (right) side of the road at the bridge, there is now a public boat launch.

Enrollments in the CCC were for six months at a time. These men have completed their first enrollment and are ready to board the train to head home to Rhode Island.

These happy men are on the way home on the Maine Central Railroad, seen here leaving Oquossoc. Many would re-enroll for another six months.

DISCOVER THOUSANDS OF LOCAL HISTORY BOOKS FEATURING MILLIONS OF VINTAGE IMAGES

Arcadia Publishing, the leading local history publisher in the United States, is committed to making history accessible and meaningful through publishing books that celebrate and preserve the heritage of America's people and places.

Find more books like this at
www.arcadiapublishing.com

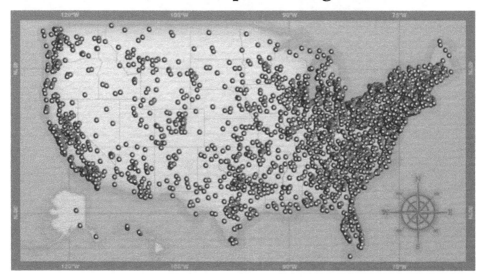

Search for your hometown history, your old stomping grounds, and even your favorite sports team.

Lightning Source UK Ltd.
Milton Keynes UK
UKHW010423260422
402057UK00004B/75